CHRISTMAS
Greetings

To   John,
with best wishes
for Christmas.
From Dorina.

Merry England, etc.

RONALD SEARLE

Merry England, etc.

PERPETUA BOOKS

First Published by
PERPETUA LTD.,
32 Newton Road,
London W.2
and distributed for them by
MICHAEL JOSEPH LTD.,
26 Bloomsbury Street,
London W.C.1

1956

ACKNOWLEDGEMENTS

A number of the drawings in this book are reproduced by courtesy of the NEWS CHRONICLE and TIME AND TIDE, in whose pages they originally appeared.

For permission to include material previously published in PUNCH, my thanks are due to the Proprietors.

The remaining drawings, I hasten to add, are new.

R.S.

For
Kaye
Kate & John

"*Now let's see what happens . . .*"

"Flippin' Mithras heads"

Rumblings of Spring in Paris

Come, fill the Cup, and in the Fire of Spring
The Winter Garment of Repentance fling:
  The Bird of Time has but a little way
to fly — and Lo! the Bird is on the Wing.

Omar Khayyám

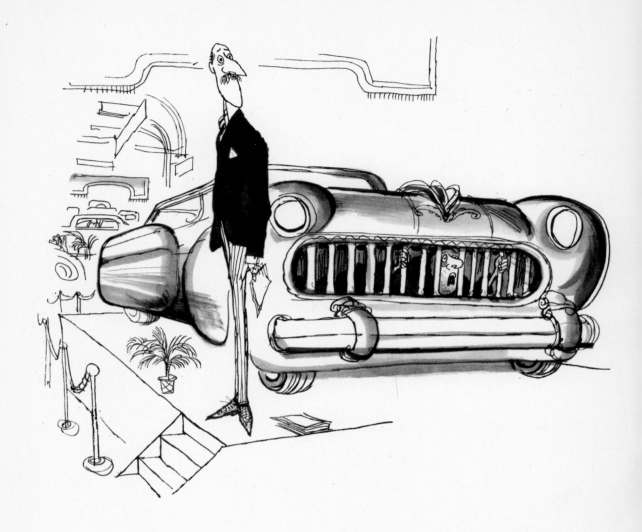

Yours in haste

Your most obedient servant

Your loving son

Yours ever

Yours sincerely

Cordially yours

Yours till the cows come home

Yours faithfully

Man's best friend

"Racing results up yet?"

" . . . and don't point, it's rude "

May I have the pleasure?

33

How to kill a man . . .

In six efforts

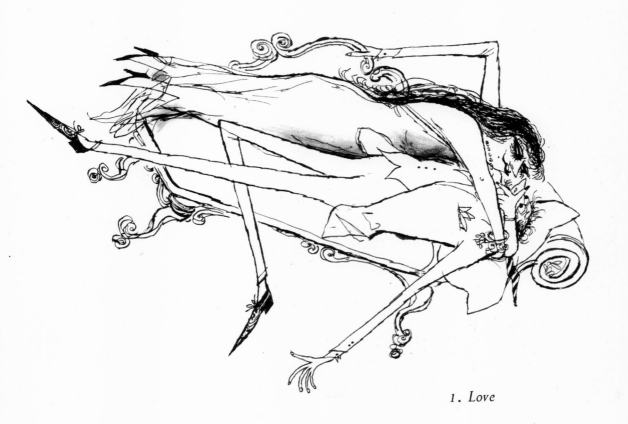

1. Love

2. Jealousy

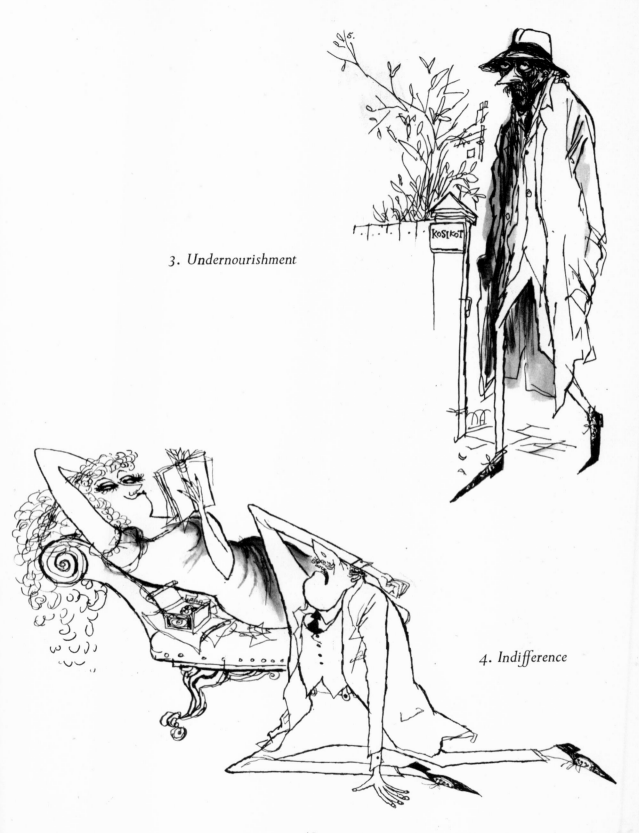

3. *Undernourishment*

4. *Indifference*

5. *Poison*

6. *Pure strength*

"Unaccountable thing, heredity . . ."

The Child-hater

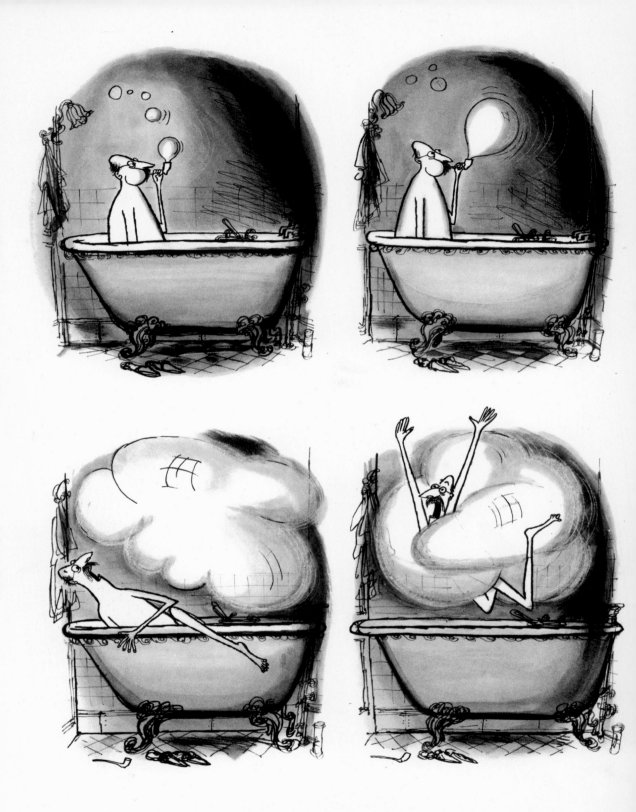

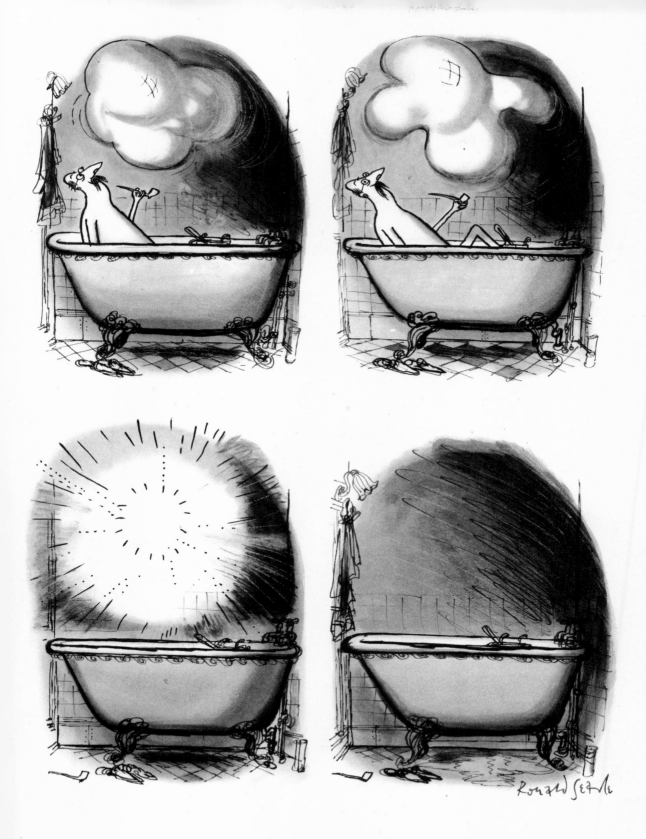

"Sorry!"

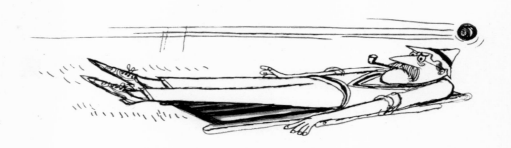

Ronald Searle 1954
Wimbledon

"Liar!"

"I was born like it"

'Normal service will be resumed
as soon as possible'

'Mrs H is a real good sort'

'A home from home'

'I feel a different man'

'I shall certainly
be back next year'

'Her rock cakes are marvellous'

" I say, I think it's going to clear"

"Looks like mutiny . . ."

"I'm afraid it's the weather"

"I'm afraid it's the weather"

"How much is this one?"

"*Do as you are told
and come out!*"

*"Well I told you
to bring a mac"*

"But darling, my feet are killing me"

Exhibition of Flemish Art
1300–1700
Royal Academy of Arts

Royal Academy
RESTAURANT

Charles I: Van Dyck

Good god!

Jan Fyt

Searle, Burlington House Dec.53

An old favourite . . .

Private View at the
Royal Academy

'Sharp pains, doctor—
just here in my knee. . .'

"Waiter! could I have a fork, please?"

'A Senator McCarthy to see you, Sir'

'*Dear Mummy . . .*'

Christmas day in the Workhouse: variations on a theme

with apologies to Gr.h.m S.th.rl.nd

Gone for
Questioning
Back at 3.0

The Society of Marine Conchologists makes its greatest discovery

Everything must go

The Spirit of Autumn

"Oh, please, not yet
not yet . . ."

Soothing the savage breast

The Harpy

Ronald Searle

The pipes!
The pipes!

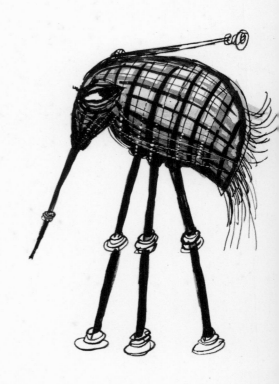

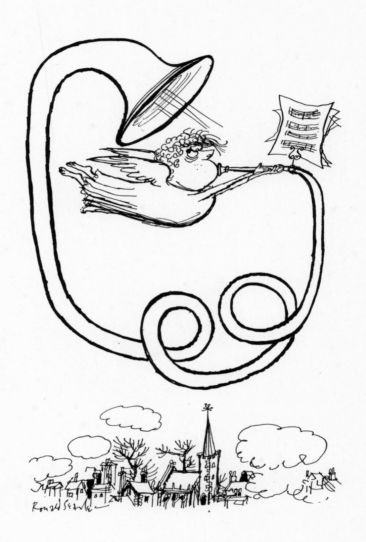

The hand of Authority

The End